DO ASK, DO TELL

DATING GUIDE

I0123330

A ROMANTIC REVOLUTION EDITION

BY
CHRISTINA CHEMHURU
(M.B.A.)

FOREWARD

BY

DR. MYLES MUNROE

Do Ask Do Tell
The Romantic Revolution ~ Dating Guide

Published by Christina Chemhuru (MBA)
Copyright © 2013 by Christina Chemhuru (MBA)

Or at the email address or websites below.
www.doaskdotellbooks.com
http://twitter.com/DoAskDoTellBook.com
http://facebook.com/Krystyn777
www.christinachemhuru.com
ceo@christinachemhuru.com
To order go to https://www.createspace.com/4384761

Scripture quoted from the King James Version Bible
Printed in the United States of America
Library of Congress Cataloging-in-Publication data
Writer's Guild of America West
Chemhuru, Christina.

Do Ask, Do Tell: The Romantic Revolution ~ Dating Guide.
        Includes index and foreward
        Includes preface by Dr. Myles Munroe
        Cover image and design by Christina Chemhuru
(MBA)
Title ID: 4384761
ISBN-13: 978-0615904009
ISBN-10: 0615904009
1. The main category of the book —Dating, relationship
Another subject category —The Romantic Revolution 3.
More categories —A Dating Guide. 4. And their modifiers.
I. Chemhuru, Christina. (MBA) II. Title. III. Subtitles
First Edition

14 13 12 11 10 / 10 9 8 7 6 5 4 3 2 1

I count not myself to have apprehended, but this one thing I do; forgetting those things which are behind, and reaching forth unto those which are before, I press toward the mark for the prize of the high calling of God in Jesus Christ

Philippians 3: 13-14 (KJV)

Do Ask, Do Tell

The Romantic Revolution Collection

Also by this Author

Do Ask, Do Tell Dating Guide

Do Ask, Do Tell Workbook

Do Ask, Do Tell Blog

Do Ask, Do Tell TV & Radio Show

Email: admin@DoAskDoTellBooks.com

Website: www.DoAskDoTellBooks.com

Twitter: www.twitter.com/DoAskDoTellBook

Facebook: www.facebook.com/DoAskDoTellBooks

Website: www.ChristinaChemhuru.com

BOOKS ALSO AVAILABLE FOR SALE ON THIS CREATESPACE LINK

www.createspace.com/4384761

Dedicated to the God

Who has loved me through it all

And the remarkable women He has on

His team

~ * ~

My Mother ~ **Joyce Chemhuru**

My Twin Sister ~ **Katherine Manase**

My Pastor – **Maureen Shana**

My Lifelong Best Friend – **Joyce Mkushi**

~ * ~

Walking alongside me has been eventful

to say the least, but for love and laughter

you have stuck around and for that,

I love and thank you all.

Here's to each of you for the past 20

years, and counting and for the lifetime

ahead.

CONTENTS

NOTE FROM THE AUTHOR

The Do Ask, Do Tell ~ The Romantic Revolution products are intended for a mature audience and as such the nature of the topics and the details contained in them are not all suitable for young persons. Parental guidance is advised.

This book and other products are written by a Christian woman but intended for a much wider audience not limited by race, religion, or any demographic factor that makes us beautifully unique.

There is no ridiculing, or gratuitous mentioning of sex, sexual activities, experiences, fantasies or sexual preferences in this book or any other products.

The Do Ask, Do Tell ~ The Romantic Revolution products serve as guides and tools. The nature of some of the questions will undoubtedly raise eyebrows. The elaboration of the rationale behind their inclusion should help guide you. Some actual experiences and findings in these sections will hopefully bring about some enlightenment.

May the results bring you greater joy, understanding, compassion, patience and healing so that you will learn to understand yourself from the past going onwards. I hope that you really come to terms with what you can handle and find it in you to grow beyond that. I pray that you will realize that the people you love may have endured more than you can presently handle in your life and that you are challenged to still love them. May this experience enable you to encourage others, and ultimately, may you finally let go of it and begin a new life together.

May *you* also forget... what lies behind - forgive yourself, learn to laugh at yourself and then invite us to join in the laughter. May you too press on! ☺

ꟼOREWARD BY DR. MYLES MUNROE

This erudite, eloquent, and immensely thought-provoking work gets to the heart of the deepest passions and aspirations of the human heart – have a good healthy and fulfilling relationship.

This is indispensable reading for anyone who wants to understand some of the principles of developing the foundations of good relationships in life. This is a profound authoritative work which spans the wisdom of the ages and yet breaks new ground in its approach and will possibly become a classic in this and the next generation.

This exceptional work by Christina is one of the most profound, practical, principle-centered approaches to the subject on relationships and dating I have read in a long time. The author's approach to this timely and critical issue of relationships brings a fresh breath of air that captivates the heart, engages the mind and inspires the spirit of the reader.

The author's ability to leap over complicated theological and metaphysical jargon and reduce complex theories to simple practical relationship principles that the least among us can understand is amazing.

This work will challenge the intellectual while embracing the laymen as it dismantles the mysterious of the soul search of mankind and delivers the profound in simplicity.
Christina's approach awakens in the reader the untapped inhibitors that retard our personal relationship, overcome our past hurts and develop wisdom for future success in relating to others. Christina's personal antidotes empower us to rise above

these self-defeating, self-limiting factors to a life of exploits in spiritual and mental advancement.

The author also integrates into each chapter the time-tested precepts giving each principle a practical application to life making the entire process people-friendly.

Every sentence of this book is pregnant with wisdom and I enjoyed the mind-expanding experience of this exciting book. I admonish you to plunge into this ocean of knowledge and watch your life change for the better as you experience a future of success in your relationships.

Dr. Myles Munroe
BFM International
ITWLA
Nassau Bahamas

PREFACE

Dating is no longer what it used to be, from many perspectives. We live in a society that is immensely sexually charged. Where couples limit or completely forgo connecting on an intellectual and emotional level until they have managed to know each other in a physical or intimate way. Many place a much greater importance on exhausting their sexual curiosity about each other first.

The argument being, in most cases, that it is necessary to establish "sexual compatibility". So countless couples co-habit, engage or marry without knowing more than the template details of their partners' online profile. Yet they wonder why they cannot deal with discovering who the "real person" is that they are committed to. Then after the honeymoon is over they often accuse them of changing.

Often couples consider a series of fun-filled dates to the movies, romantic dinners, concerts, sports games and even religious gatherings as being the ultimate way to spend "quality time" with a loved one. Recreation in dating is essential, healthy and beneficial but exploring one's mate from a more intellectual and conversational angle would add more value to the relationship in both the short and long run.

So how could one get more acquainted with the person of their fancy where time may be limited and first impressions are often unreliable? Re-read their online profile? Stalk them? Peruse their resume? Run a background check? Ask around about them? Some of these could help but at best they would barely scratch the surface and at worst give a distorted image of the person being studied. So perhaps the best approach would be to begin to incorporate some pertinent questions into the conversation.

Of course one may have already employed this strategy several times from the initial meeting until this stage. Asking questions like, "What is your favorite color or food?" and "What is your dream vacation or holiday destination?" and "What do you like about your job?" Or simply, "tell me more about yourself". These are necessary small talk and ice-breakers but do not stop there.

Questions should be posed that can allow one to see their mate's life from a bird's eye view. There are those that help gain an understanding of one's history; the experiences that have defined them and influenced their principles and persuasions. Then there are questions that enable them to comfortably reveal their present state; their current mental, emotional, physical health and financial disposition. Not excluding their reflections on critical matters such as politics, marriage, divorce, monogamy, pre-marital sex and abortion.

Other areas may include religion, tithing, prayer and fasting, how to raise children, finances, pre-nuptial agreements, spending habits, debt and budgeting, and conflict resolution. These are just some of the areas that may need to be covered to establish the level of commonality or consensus already existing between couples. This will also help to discern which pivotal areas may affect the future of the relationship if disparity exists.

All these areas require effective tools that assist in exploring a person, their spouse/partner and the relationship at hand as well as in roughly predetermining, what a future with this person could entail.

This book does not attempt or recommend psycho-analyzing a potential mate. Rather it gives the tools with which to help discover *together* who one's mate once was, who they are at present and who they are likely to become. Especially if one might have or would like to have the privilege of being a part of that transformation or their future.

This process does not remain one-sided though. It is hardly possible for the one seeking answers to not share and discover quite a bit about themselves too, during the same process.

For those who have already tied the knot and carried each other across the threshold, it would be strongly recommended to first read this *entire* book whilst making notes in the workbook. Then reflect on which areas are most pertinent to the health and survival of the marriage before raising them with the help of Do Ask, Do Tell Workbook.

One must determine how much they <u>need</u> to know and if they can handle the likely responses. Lack of preparation in addressing whatever issues may additionally arise may prove counter-effective. Poor planning may even result in detriment to not only the relationship, but to each other's self-esteem and your ability to open up on future occasions.

Much care, caution and empathy must be applied especially when the information being shared is startling, shocking, disturbing or confusing.

Confidentiality must NEVER be breached even if the person sharing seems light-hearted about the information, or they volunteer it *seemingly* without reluctance. Sometimes humor or minimization is employed as a coping mechanism and should not be taken at face value.

When a person shares their personal information with another, usually a certain level of trust has already been developed in their relationship. Allow them therefore, to have the right and privilege to develop *that same level of trust* with the next person they choose to share their personal details with. Assume nothing. Ask for permission before divulging any information. As someone finally shares a burden that they have carried for what seems to be an eternity, the weight of confidentiality is shared. It is necessary to emphasize it so much, be worthy of their trust.

Be sympathetic and listen. Do not be judgmental. Suspend judgment for as long as possible and if you become uneasy with the information shared, discuss it. Pretending it does not affect you when it does creates under currents that eventually affect other areas of your relationship. Soon nuances and attitude problems will begin to seep dangerously into your relationship. Realize that the problem or challenge may not be so much **what** the other person had to reveal, but *your* difficulty in hearing or accepting it.

Do realize also that though this process could open up old wounds, it could also bring healing and closure to hurts that have been carried for a long time. Poor timing or insensitivity in dealing with the issues that arise could result in impeding the healing process, if not furthering the damage previously done.

Conducting these exercises well could result in immeasurable; increased trust, closeness, bonding and a greater understanding of each other. The shared experiences will help in being better prepared to love the "whole package" more freely. Couples could grow together in more compassionate and supportive ways. Even if the romantic relationship fails, a tremendous, lasting and loyal friendship would have been re-created.

If some questions are awkward or embarrassing to ask and you fear being judged as strange for raising such a question, do not worry; you can always use the excuse that "it was in the book!"

Remember, this is NOT the Great Inquisition. Have fun!!!

ꟿNTRODUCTION

There are many motives to question before going out seeking the intimate details of another person's life. If your intention is not to create a deeper bond with the person, then avoid asking the most intimate personal details from them or disclosing yours to them until the relationship mutually warrants that development. Both of you must feel safe in order for this to work well.

Understand that the more intimate the details shared, the closer the bond that is developed or suggested. Therefore, avoid attempting to bond with someone to *that* extent without considering and establishing if such a development to the relationship is mutually beneficial and mutually desired. The same applies with pastors, counselors and even human resource managers; a choice has to be consciously made to decide if sharing such details is in fact in one's best interest, particularly if it is one-sided.

Before embarking on this exploration, read this book in its entirety. At the end it will be much easier to establish which "new information" would adversely affect a relationship if it were only discovered or revealed much later. Then decide how and when to best broach these delicate topics. Use the Do Ask, Do Tell Workbook to bookmark, tab or highlight the sections, or questions that are of interest and attempt to answer them *truthfully* <u>yourself</u> before posing them to your partner.

This will help you to assess your readiness to approach these topics as well as to decide which areas may not be in the best interest of your relationship at this stage. The later chapters in this book will help you to develop, appreciate and nurture your partner better. If certain sections or chapters are uncomfortable for either of you, you could consider revisiting them later.

Here's to a journey of discovery, of self and of others. May those who take this expedition find more understanding, self-fulfillment, empowerment and joy in love and life. May their understanding reside more "in the moment" than in hind-sight. May the healing and freedom found in loving someone special come no longer at a high price but may you find that the truth does indeed set you free.

May dating be what it once was and really ought to be ~ a beautiful opportunity to grow to know someone and embrace them – their past, present and future - in truth, compassion and in the strength and safety of this newfound knowledge. And when your love has endured and conquered its initial trials, may it lead to a marriage in which your hearts will grow and be safer to love and safer in love. May you have fewer surprises.

CHAPTER ONE

WHAT LIES IN A QUESTION?

Well, the answer, for one. When talking with people whom we've just met or whom we would like to know on a deeper level, we investigate them by observing them or simply asking questions. We have a need to quickly determine whether we like, or feel safe around that person or not. So the "friendliest" mannerisms like smiling back or making small talk or even a handshake make us feel that we can safely predict their behavior and temperament. The same goes for unfriendly behavior. The more time we spend around people the more likely we are to use any new information to confirm our first impressions and further project into their personalities and our relationship with them.

In a group setting, people who don't open up or give us something to work with perplex us because we feel a need to make a decision about them right away. The instant they open up to even one person a decision is reached instantly and fed to the group. Even if we never personally get a chance to engage them in a discussion, we already know how we feel about them. We need to determine who is a friend and who is a foe. Its basic survival.

Romantic relationships are no different. We give ourselves a certain time frame in which to decide if we want to know someone better. We are content as long as that person is consistent with our initial impression and no new negative information comes to light. When this length of time or series of events have passed we make a permanent decision about the relationship. Sadly, the quest to purposefully discover more about the other person is also abandoned and we are comfortable with what we have assumed, confirmed and discovered this far. The rest will be a surprise!

The questions in this book do not seek to make you doubt everyone you know but rather make you develop a better approach to getting to know them. They guide you to base your relationship more on who you both are than on your assumptions and projections. You will get there by asking the right questions. Be ready for *absolutely any* and every possible response.

This is crucial. Start by asking *yourself* the upcoming questions to help determine whether you <u>need</u> to know the information you are asking for and *if* you are prepared to hear it. When not prepared for the responses we receive we are often shocked, tend to over-react or escalate the situation. A lot of damage can occur.

The fact is you are not always going to hear what you expect. Try some exercises with your friends and give each other unlikely responses and discuss how supportively, or not you handled them. Be honest. Participate in our blog and join a community of people that are serious about meaningful, lasting relationships. You are not alone.

INTROSPECTION

When obtaining an answer, any answer in fact; whether we consider it to be right or wrong; true or false; ambiguous or clear; expected or unexpected or even one that is embarrassing or causes unease, one usually finds themselves being asked some questions too. Such as, why do *you* want to know? Why do you ask? What is it *exactly* that you want to know? Is it really any of your business? What will you do with this information? What does the past have to do with anything? What does that have to do with *us now*? What does that change? Do you really need to know that? Can I <u>trust</u> you with such information? As so on.

These questions are fair and ought to be addressed in order to give the reassurance the other person is seeking. Better still they may be a sign that the relationship is not yet at the stage to consider your questions as appropriate. It may be best to later progress towards the more difficult questions gradually as the relationship grows in commitment from both parties. In so doing, trust has already been established and there is less resistance to share based on the mutual understanding of where the relationship is headed.

We may all have heard of people who deliberately withheld information in a relationship that they *knew* the other person would have wanted to know. They may have done so fearing that if it was ever discovered the relationship would be over. This is manipulation and it is not easy to forgive. Sometimes poor advice, lack of courage, insecurity, fear or waiting for the "perfect time" makes us look deceitful.

Just like you, your partner has the right to choose to be with you or not. It is difficult to compel someone to suddenly divulge decades of secrets and it may not even be necessary in your relationship. The questions in this book are not merely seeking out dark secrets, but are equipping you to gain a better understanding of your mate. Yes there may be some questions either of you will not be able or willing to answer. It is up to the both of you to decide whether to come back to them when you are better prepared, or to leave them out entirely.

WHAT AM I FEELING?

For now, let's start with the easy stuff; the object of your affection. This is a little exercise in honesty to begin to prepare you for the work ahead. Ask yourself how honestly you can tell apart your feelings for someone. How often have all these felt like love to you?

Attraction

- People can be physically, mentally, spiritually, sexually, emotionally, professionally, financially, politically, powerfully, socially, or even vocally attractive. Finding someone attractive is not a bad thing, but if that is the cornerstone of your relationship, be aware that any kind of attractiveness or appeal can change, anytime!

- Therefore, how important is it that this attraction lasts?

- Is there more to this feeling or is this the strongest and only identifiable emotion?

Infatuation

- A passing fancy that is all consuming while it lasts. It seldom needs to even know anything substantial about the other person.

- Do I know enough about the good and bad of the person to say it is a possibly stronger emotion than infatuation?

Gratitude

- Very similar to hero worship. You may be using one or more acts of kindness to project onto the person what their other qualities are like. What actions have you observed *consistently* in order for you attribute those qualities to them? Do you tend to amplify their good side and ignore their bad?

- Or do you choose to love them as fair exchange for what they have done for you or your loved ones?

- Persons who are supportive or assist someone during a very difficult or traumatic experience are often risk of being seen in the halo effect.

This would include but is not limited to parents, mentors, close friends, spouses, coaches, counselors and teachers. They are often surprised to learn that the recipient of their generosity has developed an attachment or romantic feelings for them.

- One major unpleasant or negative revelation could change those feelings drastically. Like discovering the feelings aren't mutual. What would change everything for you?

Excitement

- Relocating, a new job, new campus, being single again, joining dating communities and traveling all get us stirred up with the excitement of meeting "someone" new.

  The exciting intrigue of any amiable stranger can sweep us off our feet and make us feel that they must be special if we feel like this.

- Feeling this way *each* time we see them could create confusion. Yet when the novelty and excitement have worn off, what feelings remain?

Lust

- Having *only* a desire to connect on a physical level shows that the other person appeals to us in an erotic manner.
  When you spend together, what are you doing? Do you have a healthy balanced lifestyle to your relationship or

does one activity dominate? Is it a short-term relationship?

- Lust is relatively easy to satisfy – what remains thereafter begs justifying. It is often something made up of guilt, disappointment and sense of failure to have gained the other persons' true admiration and commitment.

- Sometimes we deny the fact that we really desire more from the relationship but more was never available.

Sympathy

- This is sadly a great motivator for people to find themselves in a relationship. They feel sorry for the other person. They feel they deserve a chance, or a break.

Look how their ex treated them, they deserve better. After all, they can't be so bad. Poor thing... widowed, divorced, single parent and still they believe in love. How admirable.

- Or the tireless suitor. They have always loved me or pursued me endlessly so they must truly love me. Let me meet them halfway. Let me just give it a shot.

- Sadly when the reason we felt sorry for someone no longer exists, so too does the rationale for staying become meaningless.

- Then either we leave or we feel too sorry for them that we stay again, out of sympathy.

Love

- You know as much good about them as bad and still want to be with them and love them.

- You have endured times' tests and trials and survived. Only love can survive, where all the others above never make it.

- You have a friendship whose bond is more eternal than the attraction.

- You share a vision and a dream for each other's' future. You bring out the best and the worst in each other and still choose to be in the relationship.

These are just a few indicators of each emotion. You should be able to now list or identify your own signs of each emotion.

If you are convinced that you want to, or are ready to build a future with someone you will need to ask yourself some serious questions.

- Does the present nature of the relationship or the feelings I have necessitate getting to know them better? Does the other person feel the same way?

- Do I think I can be or should be trusted with their answers?

- Can I be trusted with the truthful response - that I won't use it against this person to violate their trust or hurt them?

- Can I handle the responses I get, both expected and unexpected?

- What if I get what I consider to be a "wrong" or undesirable answer?

- What if I get angry or they do? What next?

- What if either of us feels cheated or disappointed because they are finding out certain facts only now? Or they feel guilty for what they have disclosed? How will we get past this?

- What if the other person discloses criminal or illegal activities in their past, what should I do?

- What if the answer is something I cannot deal with, am I prepared to keep this relationship going?

- Why do I really feel I <u>need</u> to know all this?

- Am I able to respect the answer I hear and treat it with the gravity it deserves?

- What if I don't believe the answer to be the truth, should I keep pursuing the issue?

- What if I cannot readily get an answer – is delay tantamount to denial/refusal?

- What if an answer or explanation is denied?

- What will a refusal to respond mean to me?

- What if either of us believes certain things should remain secrets for the health of the relationship? Should we maintain our ground?

- What if the other person believes in full disclosure, does that mean I can never keep certain things to myself, even things told to me in confidence?

- Will these answers help me make more important decisions?

- Is there a better or "best time" to ask this question, is so, can it wait?

- Do I really need clarity or is this just curiosity?

- If I was asked the same or a similar question what would <u>my</u> answer be?

- What if I am unable or unwilling to answer the same question, should I still ask it if it's important to me?

- Would the same question offend or upset me? How would it make me feel?

- What if I don't know how to interpret the answer, should I ask someone else or will that be a violation of this person's trust in me?

- My relationship is going great, why ruin a good thing?

I strongly recommend that each of the persons doing this exercise read the book in its entirety and then agree on which boundaries they will set and how they will deal with some of the more difficult scenarios listed above. Assume nothing and if the other is unable or unwilling to answer any question, confirm with them if they would like to revisit the question later or just skip it altogether. It may not be advisable or necessary to probe for the reason, even if one of you was able to answer the question with ease.

CHAPTER TWO

ICE-BREAKER QUESTIONS

Now try using these questions when meeting someone for the first time and you need some ice-breakers that get the conversation going, or even with old friends. They are fun and challenge people to think about themselves in ways they may have never done so before. If someone is dominating the conversation, either out of nervousness or excitement, these questions can help share the air-space when they turn the questions on each other.

Please do not forget to ask the other person the same questions. I have had several people fail to do this. Although understandable to a certain extent, it may come across as though one is full of themselves and have no interest in getting to know about the other person.

That said, let me emphasize again that *in my opinion* there is no right or wrong answer for everyone. One must make their own decision based on their preferences. In fact, to understand why there is no "right or wrong" answer as such, pose these questions to your family and friends and see the variety of responses they yield. Remember that not all these are everyday questions so not many people will be able to give an answer right away, they may need to think about it for a while.

If an entire section remains unanswered, I suggest you come back to it after a day or two before you proceed to the next phase. This is because the sections get into more personal and deep issues. Without the ease of transition the chapters give, probing into deeper issues could prove shocking, embarrassing. This could even more unfortunately create a 'block' or barrier that makes the parties unwilling to participate any further in this process.

This first section helps to get an idea of how big someone's' dream are. What power, talents and abilities they secretly wish to possess, whether you are aware of them or not. Try to avoid over-psychoanalyzing. Most people struggle to think of their best answer right away and settle for the first thing they think of. For this reason one should also avoid prompting or suggesting possible answers. They may just pick from what you mention.

To the women let me say that I have found that when posing the "opposite gender" questions some men get uncomfortable and refuse to answer. If you get the same or similar response, don't fret. When they ask you the same questions and you answer, they may become comfortable enough to go back and answer them. If not, leave out those particular ones and proceed. I do not deem them to be harmful questions so avoid insisting where it's not necessary. This is a two part question so do let them explain <u>their</u> reasons for their choice of answer. Make sure the "why?" part of each question is answered and elaborated on where necessary.

So, to get the conversation started you can bring up the following questions and see where they take you.

- What is your present occupation?

- If you did not need to work for money, what would you choose to do and why?

- Which was your best job ever and why?

- Which was your worst job ever and why?

- If you were an animal, which one would you be and why?

- If you were a bird, which one would you be and why?

- If you <u>had</u> to be any other person on earth (dead/alive) who would it be and why?

Let us assume you retained your gender in the previous questions.

- If you were an animal of the opposite gender, if different, which one would you be and why?

- If you were a bird of the opposite gender, if different, which one would you be and why?

- If you <u>had</u> to be any other person on earth, of the opposite gender (dead/alive) who would it be and why?

- Do you consider yourself as being ambitious? Explain why or why not?

- Do you consider yourself to be accomplished? Explain.

- If you are comfortable sharing your dreams, describe when you were a child, what you dreamt of being as an adult.

- If that dream changed describe the dreams that took its place

In the event that the conversation has become very intense and serious, you could wrap this section up with something light hearted, like;

- Do you dream in color, black and white, hues of blue, green, sepia etc.? Please recount a dream you recall in one of these colors.

If for question 3 they give a bird or an insect as an answer to which animal they would be, try to encourage them to think of an actual animal as they are different to birds. For instance, if you were trying to think of the strongest animal, it would be very different from what you think the strongest bird would be. Often I have heard people say, "I can't think of any bird, mention a few for me". The danger in this is that they will make a selection based on what you offered them and not from the creatures that made the greatest impression on them or those that they identify with. Avoid, in fact do not prompt any answers or offer examples.

Human beings have amazing capabilities that animals do not have. Yet we envy and even fantasize about being certain creatures because of certain flairs and traits they exhibit. Most people covet their sizes, ability to move, run, fight, hunt, and nurture and protect their young. Birds and animals defend their territory with skills that leave us in awe.

For example, many people would like to be a tiger but their reasons vary. Some say because it is a big beautiful creature, others say because it is the king of the jungle, and others because they perceive it to be strong. The reasons differ from person to person. One may be appalled by the same response that would generate admiration elsewhere. The animal qualities we wish we had could suggest in what areas we either feel we excel naturally in or that we lack the most in.

Desiring to be a tiger may mean to some that the person saying this feels that they are big, beautiful, dominant and strong.

Another may interpret this to say maybe they in fact feel weak and unattractive and wish they could change all that.

Others have said horses, dolphins and other animals I love and as such I may find myself more approving of them at that point. That is, until they state their reasons why. It is necessary to ask "why?" Their reasoning is more important than your assumption. Hence I say there is no right or wrong answer. Just observe how their answer resonates with you. It does say something about you too.

Remember to try not to psychoanalyze. It is tempting and when patterns begin to emerge you may be tempted to believe that you have "cracked the code". Keep going and enjoy being blown away.

CHAPTER THREE

DEAL BREAKERS

This next stage is for when both parties have become comfortable enough to discuss having a serious relationship. The questions in this chapter will help them determine whether a relationship has a chance or not, long before any emotions are invested in it. If any of these issues here are deal breakers for you, it is all the more reason to find out as early as possible where your potential mate stands with regards to these matters.

That said, there will be other questions in the rest of the book that may also constitute deal breakers for you. In the interest of creating a gradual progression from less delicate subjects to more intimate ones, the ones in the later chapters are best brought up much later. Remember to create a disturbance-free and comfortable environment before you begin. Expect to become vulnerable but remain honest in what you decide to share or decide not to share.

- You have just started seeing or dating someone. What would you consider to be a deal breaker that would cause you to stop seeing them if you found out about it?

- Why would you see this as a deal breaker or seriously consider ending the relationship over this?

- You have been steadily or seriously dating someone for some time, and may have become committed to them. At this stage, what would be a deal breaker for you?

- Why would you see this as a deal breaker or seriously consider ending the relationship over this?

- If you are a woman ask, "Have you ever been hit *by* a woman?"

- If you are a man ask, "Have you ever hit a man?"

- What had happened? Narrate the whole incident and how it ended.

- If you are a woman now ask, "Have you ever *hit* a woman?"

- If you are a man now ask, "Have you ever been hit *by* a man?"

- What had happened? Narrate the whole incident and how it ended.

- Describe how your most significant relationships started and how they ended.

- Describe the nature of the relationships you have been able to maintain with any of the people from your previous relationships?

- Are you interested in a monogamous relationship at this stage?

- At which point do you think a dating couple should become exclusive?

- Define exclusive.

- Are you currently involved with anyone or still in love or emotionally involved with someone? Please explain

- Are you aware of anyone actively perusing a relationship with you, whether or not you are interested in them? If so, please elaborate?

- Please provide information on any of the persons you ever had relationships with who are still problematic or giving you undesired attention.

- Have either you or any of your previous partners ever called the police, filed charges or obtained a restraining order on you, whether the matter was later dropped, or solved between the two of you?

- Describe the events that led to this.

- Describe any situations that escalated and required intervention or assistance to contain them.

- If any children or relatives were involved please explain how

- Do you or are you involved in any capacity in any legal cases before a court of law? Have you considered all legal matters, personal, business, civil, criminal, federal etc.? Please provide details of any cases.

- What is your position/principle/opinion on each of the following issues as regarding dating, relationships and marriage?

  - Current marital status

  - Cheating

  - Monogamy

  - Marriage

  - Co-habitation

  - Divorce

  - Politics or political affiliations

  - Social lifestyle

  - Sexual lifestyle

- Children

- Dependents – family members

- Medical health and history

- Physical fitness/attractiveness

- Dietary habits

- Past and current addictions

- Use of drugs, alcohol and tobacco

- Gambling

- Financial stability/savings

- Debt

- Credit score

- Pre-nuptial agreements

- Divorce

- Job stability

- Education level/background

- Criminal history

- Cleanliness

- Personal Hygiene

As this list is not exhaustive, feel free to bring up any other topics that can be accommodated with the same level of openness. These topics are basic but necessary conversation pieces which should give some indication of the degree of adjusting they would need to make if living with this person.

These are general relational topics so have fun with them. There really is no need for any of these to become heated arguments or debates. The idea is to get a feel of the "small things" that matter to the other person.

These can also potentially be both deal-breakers as well as pet peeves. Being upfront as this stage can let the other person know if a relationship would or not succeed. It will be very beneficial to cover these questions over the initial meetings or dates and certainly before being intimate with each other. It would make walking away or deciding to be just friends much easier.

CHAPTER FOUR

YOU - THE REAL YOU

This chapter is a welcome adaptation of the well-intended interview question, "Tell me about yourself." What the question seeks to do is to give the person responding a platform from which to introduce themselves, show off a little bit and admit to some faults. This question may yield much better responses in a dating scenario than an interview. Nonetheless, here is a less agonizing and bite-sized approach to asking what you what to know.

Have no doubts that some extremely unexpected content could be shared at this point. Make every effort to control and contain your shock, rage or even laughter as any unexpected reaction may inadvertently cause embarrassment, resentment and possibly rejection. Allow both parties time to adjust to the new information and if necessary, be prepared to allow them to leave.

- What is your personal philosophy on life, if you have one?

- What is your life's purpose?

- How would you best describe yourself?

- How would your friends describe you?

- Describe what you believe are your finer qualities

- What are your life's greatest achievements?

- Which areas are you not so proud about and if so, how have you tried to change them?

- What makes you angry?

- What do you do when you get really angry?

- Have you ever had reason to regret your actions when you were angry?

- How challenging do you find it to forgive people?

- What do you consider to be unforgivable?

- Describe a time when you were able to successfully payback someone for having wronged you.

- How do you get along with all or most of your family members?

- Do you have any enemies? Explain how they came about.

- Describe situations in which you feel most vulnerable?

- At what times do you tend to feel lonely?

- How do you handle loneliness?

- How easily do you make friends?

- How easy is it for you to trust people?

- Do you have any close friends and how well do you feel you know each other?

- How would your friends describe you?

- How would your co-workers describe you?

- How might this be different from how your family members describe you?

- To what extent does your family and friends' approval or opinions of your partner or date affect your choice to commit to them?

- Has this always been the case? Please explain your answer.

- Do you have any extremities to your personality that you are either personally aware of or have been told of by others? Please describe them

- In the event that it hasn't come up yet, what is the worst thing or things that you have ever done, that you wouldn't want anyone to know?

The last question really gives both persons the opportunity to confess something that their conscience or guilt would have burdened them with until this point. It is good to get this question out of the way early on and let a relationship or friendship emerge in which one feels free and totally accepted.

If they still choose to love you after knowing your response, you will love them all the more. If you withhold your true response, you will forever live in fear of the day they find out. Should that day happen, they may have every right to feel deceived, especially after having asked you this question too.

CHAPTER FIVE

CHILDHOOD AND CHILDREN

This next section deals with family and childhood issues. Explanations may get lengthy so please be patient and listen and probe for details where necessary. It is highly recommended to use open-ended questions where possible as they will yield more thorough answers that will not be limited to "yes" or "no". However, feel free to use the questions that require a simple "yes/no" when clarifying a point. Or simply invite them to explain.

FORMATIVE RELATIONSHIPS

- Who raised you? Describe the household lifestyle?

- What were your parents' educational backgrounds?

- What were their sources of income?

- Have you ever been exposed to a relationship where the woman earned a higher income than the man? Or the man stayed at home or was unemployed even if it was for a short while? If so, what did you learn, observe or appreciate from the situation and how the couple handled it?

- If you have been in this situation, describe how you handled it and in what ways you believe it affected your relationship?

- Should you find yourself in this situation in the future, how would you see yourself handling it?

- How are your current relations with your each of your parents and each sibling?

- How many siblings do you have and what are their present occupations?

- How are your siblings' relationships and marriages? Describe what you have observed about their relationships.

- Are you supportive of each other's successes and failures?

- Taking a step back, how do you feel your parents' relationships impacted you and your siblings' relationships?

- Looking at your parents, siblings' or other relationships during your youth, what resolutions did you make then about your future relationships?

DISCIPLINE, PUNISHMENT & PARENTING STYLES

- Describe your childhood? What were the most memorable moments of your childhood?

- What do you recall as being the worst or most unpleasant childhood disciplining experience?

- Please describe any experiences that you believe were abusive? How did you handle them?

- If you were ever bullied how did you handle it? Who was the perpetrator?

- Describe any incidents were you may have been in trouble at school.

- How where you punished and rewarded as a child and how do you feel about that now?

- If you were ever administered any form of corporal punishment like caning, whipping or belting, please explain who punished you and on what occasions.

- How have you resolved, managed or lived with the negative experiences surrounding your childhood disciplining?

- Have you ever spoken about these experiences with your parents/ pastors/ counselors/ relatives/ spouse or partner/ or other siblings?

- If so, what was their reaction and how did you feel about it?

- How did you respond to/ relate to persons in positions of authority when you were growing up?

- What is, or what would be your approach to disciplining children?

- What methods of punishment do you prefer for your children?

- If corporal punishment is one of them, please explain how you would administer it, when and until what age.

- What resolutions have you made or did you make when you pictured yourself as a parent based on your past?

- If you already have children describe your relationship with them?

- If you have any nephews or nieces describe your relationship with them.

- If any of your siblings have children or they desire to have any children, what parenting methods do you believe they have adopted from their upbringing?

- How do your parenting styles differ?

- If you are a parent or guardian or have frequent occasions to deal with minors, how do you believe your childhood impacts the way you relate to children now?

- As a parent or potential parent do you feel you have managed to correct or will be able to correct what errors you believe your parents made? Please explain how you did or how you propose to do so?

- If you do desire to have children, how many would you like to have?

- How near or far in the future would you like to start a family?

- Describe your relationship with the other parent or parents of your child or children if applicable.

- How involved would you like your new spouse or partner to be in raising, disciplining and mentoring your children?

- Describe your position on raising your children in a religious or non-religious home.

- What would make you reconsider starting a family with a potential spouse or partner?

- What would you say or do if your new or potential spouse or partner desired a child?

- What would you say or do if your new or potential spouse or partner did not want a child?

- If you both desired to start a family and either you or your partner was unable or unwilling to have children how would this affect your decision to stay in the relationship?

- Would adoption be an option you would be willing to consider? Please explain.

- Explain any difficulties in conceiving you have had in the past, currently have or may have in the future?

- Have you ever under gone any fertility tests and or treatments? How did this come about and what was the outcome?

- Did any pregnancies arise from any of your sexual relations? Did/do you dispute your paternity in any of these?

- If so, were any children subsequently born? Is there any question on the paternity of any of them? Explain why.

- If not, were any of these pregnancies terminated? Explain your part or knowledge of this.

- How did any pregnancies affect your relationships?

- Did any pregnancies result in a miscarriage?

- How did the loss of any pregnancies affect you? How would you handle a miscarriage or stillbirth today?

- As far as you know, did the termination of any pregnancies affect your ability to have children?

- What measures/recourse can you or have you taken if you still want to have children?

- In you or your partners' culture or belief system are you encouraged or expected to live with or have financial responsibility over your parents, siblings or any relatives? Please explain the extent of any obligations now or in the possible future?

- Do you feel you have a very strong cultural or religious background and would like to raise your children according to it? If your partner was opposed to this how would this affect you?

- How involved would you like either of your families to be in raising your children? How likely will this be?

- What are or might be the no-compromise issues regarding your preferred parenting style and explain why you feel so strongly about these issues?

- If your child declared they were interested in a same sex relationship, how would you handle this?

CHAPTER SIX

PAST AND FUTURE RELATIONSHIPS

For some people, even before their first ever relationship they have a very specific list describing their perfect mate. Others are entirely unsure and therefore very accommodating. Regardless, after a few romantic endeavors, experience teaches us all to have requirements. As we begin to know who we are and who we are not, we also begin to decide who we do and do not want in our lives.

For example, a young adult may have a list of what they want in their future spouse, but after a few heartbreaks, the list may comprise entirely of what they *don't* want. How we respond to the most recent events in our relationships affects our mindset as we go into the next one. How we respond to all our previous relationships could determine how we behave in all our future relationships too.

Understanding the imprints that past relationships left on your mate helps you to better understand them. These imprints are both good and bad and set standards for future relationships. Dismissing everything from the past as "baggage" is unfortunate and erroneous. Grievous as it may be to hear, someone in your partner's past may have already set a high standard for you to meet or beat. Likewise, someone may have already proved more disappointing than you could ever be. Take comfort in that.

As life's' journey is awash with love and the joys and pains that often accompany it, it is worth investing some time in understanding how you each came to have the values and ideals that for now, define you.

This section enables you to walk back in time with your loved one and vicariously relive the romantic adventures that brought them to where they are today. Enjoy the journey.

- Have you ever been in a long term relationship, or been engaged or married?

- How do you feel about possibly being in another long term relationship, engagement or marriage in the future?

- Do you or did you enjoy being in a relationship? Please elaborate.

- On average, how much time do you spend alone in-between relationships?

- What have you attempted or accomplished during this time of being single or unattached?

- What do you enjoy most about being in a relationship?

THE SIGNIFICANT PAST - THE GOOD

The following set of questions should be asked in turn for each
significant relationship before moving on to the next one.

- Identify the relationships you consider to have been significant and explain what makes these significant.

- In as far as you know did the other person also consider the relationship as being significant to them?

- What level of commitment was reached in the relationship and how long did it last?

- What are your best memories from this relationship?

- Which stage or occasions do you recall as being your happiest?

- What had the other person done and what had you done?

- How did this affect the way you viewed the other person?

- How did this affect the way you viewed the relationship and the effort you put into it?

- How did this affect the way *they* viewed the relationship and the effort *they* put into it?

- Did you or they ever attempt to, successfully or otherwise, recreate this experience in another relationship?

- If so what was the outcome and what did you learn?

- How has this affected your expectations from your future relationships or partners?

- In as far as you know, what were the other persons' best memories?

- Which stage or occasions do *you* recall as being their happiest?

- What had they done and what had you done?

- How did this affect the way *they* viewed you?

- How did this affect the way they viewed the relationship and the effort they put into it?

- How did this affect the way *you* viewed the relationship and the effort you put into it?

- Did either of you ever attempt to, successfully or otherwise, recreate this experience? If so what was the outcome and what did you learn from this?

- Has this affected your expectations from future relationships?

THE SIGNIFICANT PAST - THE BAD

*Now consider these questions for the same **significant** relationship. When the questions start to feel monotonous you can paraphrase them.*

- What are your worst memories from this past relationship?

- Which stage or stages do you recall as being your saddest?

- What had the other person done?

- What had you done?

- How did this affect the way you viewed the other person?

- How did this affect the way you viewed the relationship and the effort you put into it?

- How did this affect the way *they* viewed the relationship and the effort they put into it?

- Did you or they ever attempt to, successfully or otherwise, intentionally or otherwise, recreate this experience in another relationship?

- If so what was the outcome?

- What did you learn from this?

- How has this affected your expectations from your future relationships?

- In as far as you know, what were the other persons' worst memories?

- Which stage or stages do you recall as being their saddest?

- What had they done?

- What had you done?

- How did this affect the way they viewed you?

- How did this affect the way they viewed the relationship and the effort they put into it?

- How did this affect the way you viewed the relationship and the effort you put into it?

- Did either of you attempt to, successfully or otherwise, intentionally or otherwise, recreate this experience in another relationship?

- If so what was the outcome and what did you learn from this?

- How has this affected your expectations from your future relationships?

THE INSIGNIFICANT PAST - THE GOOD

The following questions should then be asked in turn for <u>each</u> **insignificant** *relationship before moving on to the next one.*

- Identify the relationships you consider to have been insignificant and explain what makes them insignificant.

- In as far as you know did the other person also consider the relationship as insignificant to them?

- What level of commitment was reached in the relationship and how long did it last?

- What are your best memories from this relationship?

- Which stage or occasions do you recall as being your happiest?

- What had the other person done and what had *you* done?

- How did this affect the way you viewed the other person?

- How did this affect the way you viewed the relationship and the effort you put into it?

- How did this affect the way *they* viewed the relationship and the effort they put into it?

- Did you or they ever attempt to, successfully or otherwise, recreate this experience in another relationship?

- If so what was the outcome? What did you learn from this?

- How has this affected your expectations from your future relationships?

- In as far as you know, what were the other persons' best memories?

- Which stage or occasions do you recall as being their happiest?

- What had they done and what had *you* done?

- How did this affect the way they viewed you?

- How did this affect the way they viewed the relationship and the effort they put into it?

- How did this affect the way you viewed the relationship and the effort you put into it?

- Did either of you ever attempt to, successfully or otherwise, recreate this experience in another relationship?

- If so what was the outcome? What did you learn from this?

THE INSIGNIFICANT PAST - THE BAD

*Now answer these questions for the same **insignificant** relationships*

- What are your worst memories from this past relationship?

- Which stage or stages do you recall as being your saddest?

- What had the other person done?

- What had you done?

- How did this affect the way you viewed the other person?

- How did this affect the way you viewed the relationship and the effort you put into it?

- How did this affect the way they viewed the relationship and the effort they put into it?

- Did you or they ever attempt to, successfully or otherwise, intentionally or otherwise, recreate this experience in another relationship?

- If so what was the outcome and what did you learn from this?

- How has this affected your expectations from your future relationships?

- In as far as you know, what were the other persons' worst memories?

- Which stage or stages do you recall as being their saddest?

- What had they done and what had you done?

- How did this affect the way they viewed you?

- How did this affect the way they viewed the relationship and the effort they put into it?

- How did this affect the way you viewed the relationship and the effort you put into it?

- Did you or they ever attempt to, successfully or otherwise, intentionally or otherwise, recreate this experience in another relationship?

- If so what was the outcome and what did you learn from this?

- How has this affected your expectations from you future relationships?

- Was this relationship insignificant because of these bad experiences, the good ones or for another reason? Explain.

CHAPTER SEVEN

MORE INTROSPECTION

The aftermath of a relationship is more often filled with a process of blaming, mourning and adjustment. Closure is frequently reached when some kind of negative resolve is made about individuals, relationships, in-laws, etc. The process of examining what really happened in a healthy way and one's role in it is often cut short by excuses and the need to reach an acceptable explanation to offer enquirers.

Yet if one fully digests what transpired in a healthy way, taking account of the good as well as the bad, a better understanding and awareness of self is possible. For example, instead of blaming the other person for never being available, one can say "I discovered that I don't function well in a relationship with an absentee spouse." That way, one resists the urge to solely blame one party for the failure of the relationship but they also accept their role in it. This helps them make better decisions about future relationships.

This method can be applied to all aspects of a relationship. Examples would include, but not be limited to money, trust, lifestyles, expectations, imbalance in the roles of each partner, children, exes, even in-laws.

~ 53 ~

This is why certain elements on our list of requirements in a mate or a relationship are likely to change after each relationship. Sometimes nothing is added or removed but the importance or level of priority of certain factors changes.

Lists are tricky to work with. When the list becomes lengthy, detailed and very precise a person often comes off as "picky". If the list describes everything from the former relationship it is assumed they are not "over it". It the list contains only certain categories, then they risk being perceived as "materialistic", "superficial", "and unrealistic" or they just have "issues".

Yet without a list we may lose track of who we have discovered ourselves to be and who we have discovered we need to have in our lives. We then risk returning to certain things that naturally attract us but don't work well for us.

We have now understood that both good and bad experiences may leave imprints in our lives. These imprints affect our self-perception as well as our romantic expectations and lists. Sometimes the imprints are not desirable and affect how we see others. It is worse when we are not aware of these influences and they create issues or problems in our current relationships. Our behavior becomes confusing and when we attempt to explain it nothing makes sense to anyone.

These unresolved issues from the past that lie beneath our decisions and behavior are commonly referred to as "baggage".

~ 54 ~

This term is often used to label someone's behavior in a derogatory manner and is very misleading.

If baggage is indeed representative of what someone left the previous relationship with, then anyone who has ever been in a relationship and was impacted negatively or positively by it has baggage! If someone left a relationship with a new perspective, new fears, new desires, new generalizations, new requirements, new ambitions, new intolerances etc. then they left with baggage! Yes, baggage is not always a bad thing. In fact family and friends expect us to have progressively better relationships having learnt something from the last one.

It is ideal that moving on is done in a positive and healthy way. Unfortunately, not all people leave their partners more able to trust or love or feel positive emotions in relationships. This is sad. The desired thing is to heal and grown out of that state, and onto a more positive one. Not to whittle and stay negative forever and to see all future relationships and partners through the negative past.

No one wants to always have to prove that they are not like the "bad person" in your past. It is equally hazardous to project good qualities onto future partners. This can lead to undue pressure and disappointment. To see how well you emerged from your past relationships, answer the following questions truthfully and go through the previous chapter again if necessary.

- What did you learn about the other person, both good and bad?

- What did you learn about yourself, both good and bad?

- How you believe you have changed from all these experiences?

- Did you since observed yourself to behave differently in your relationships and if so, in what ways?

- The following list is not exhaustive. Add to it as you see fit. In what ways have you become more or less;

  - Cautious or fearful,

  - Trusting or open,

  - Intolerant or firm,

  - Forgiving or easy-going

  - Independent or less dependent on the other person

  - Carefree or frugal

  - Spiritual or worldly

  - Withdrawn or free

  - Grateful or begrudging

- In what ways do you believe the other people changed during and or after their relationships with you?

- What have you ever tried to change about yourself to make a relationship work? Please explain.

- If so, was it in an area you suggested or that the other person suggested?

- What results did the attempted change bring about?

- Explain if you resented or appreciated the person and the relationship more or less after that attempt

- Did you ask the other person to make any concessions in exchange? If so, what were they? If not, why not?

CHAPTER EIGHT

FINANCIAL MATTERS

It has almost become a cliché; finances have become one of the leading causes for the breakdown of marriages around the world. Financial security can be equated with freedom, harmony and growth, empowerment and stability. In the absence of it restriction, contention, demise, hopelessness and uncertainty thrive.

Financial pressure can be brought about by many unexpected events and the lack of preparation can only make the hardship more severe. When a couple knows their ability to embrace the unexpected together, they are better prepared to weather the storms; given that certain variables are in place and controlled.

In order to assess a persons' "financial suitability" as a spouse, one may consider their assets, income streams, spending patterns, lifestyles and saving habits. This gives them an idea of the degree of "financial stability" they can expect from them. When the income or wealth is substantial modern marriages have begun to rely heavily on the shelter of pre-nuptial agreements. These seek to protect their wealth and investments from opportunists or "gold-diggers" or just bitter vengeful spouses when the relationship ends. Pre-nuptial agreements tend to be a very contentious topic. Their implications are usually offensive. Tread carefully.

For those with less obvious signs of wealth like assets, businesses and enormous investments, credit scores have become for many, the "fool-proof" gauge of a financially worthy spouse. It gives them an indication of how much trouble they are currently in and how quickly they may be able to access more credit to get out of trouble.

Great caution should be exercised when using an index that may not necessarily reveal everything about an individual's financial history. That score comes about as a culmination of many things. As quickly as a family tragedy can ruin a persons' credit score, so quickly too have others been observed paying people to "fix" their scores and wipe their financial histories clean. Chronic gamblers can have records as clean as a freshman in college!

If lending institutions can't accurately predict a person's financial behavior without researching their entire financial history beyond the credit scores etc., consider including more indicators too. The following are suggested questions to help you both cover the necessary angles of your financial lives.

- What are your major sources of income?

- What is your credit score (range)?

- Please give an over-view of the highs and lows of your financial history

- Are you in any debt/garnishments? How long have you had these debts and how did you get into debt?

- How much is your debt and how do you plan to pay it off?

- Is there anyone who helps you pay your debts?

- Do you pay your taxes? Do you have arrears with the IRS?

- What are your major financial obligations, both long-term and short-term?

- Do you have any dependents? If so, whom and why?

- Do you have to pay child support or alimony to anyone? Please explain.

- If you loan any friends or family money please explain the circumstances and the amounts.

- Do you currently owe any family or friends any amount of money or assets?

- Are you surety on anyone's loan? Please explain.

- Have you ever been a victim of identity theft? Please explain

- Do you have or intend to take on any student loans?

- Describe your current retirement and savings plan?

- Do you have savings or how much are you able to set aside for savings every month?

- Are you currently saving up towards something?

- What percentage of your income is your rent and your car note and other monthly bills?

- If one of your parents or mine needed to live with us, how would we afford this?

- Have you invested in any business projects, ventures, inventions, stocks, bonds or equity in the recent years? Please explain

- Have you ever traded on the money market? Briefly describe your experiences.

- Do you have a dream, ambition or goal that you would risk *everything* for? What is it?

- Have you previously invested in a business or project on your own? Explain what happened.

- Please explain if you have been or are co-signed, co-owner, or surety on any loans, accounts, leases, business, etc.?

- Do you believe in consulting/involving your partner in all your major investment decisions?

- What course of action would you take if there was no consensus on the way forward?

CHAPTER NINE

HEALTH, SEX AND INTIMACY

The questions presented below have also been identified as potential deal-breakers or challenges. This is especially so if they are discovered or brought up much later in the course of a relationship. That said it would be very premature to ask these questions when there is no talk of exclusivity or commitment in the relationship. We ease into this section with general health questions.

- Describe your fitness or exercise routine if you have one.

- Describe your physical, emotional and mental health.

- Describe your family's history of illnesses.

- What is your personal history with illness, allergies and hospitalizations?

- Are you aware of any chronic conditions that may be hereditary or that any of your family members may be prone to?

- Please explain any diagnoses and treatments you are under-going for any medical condition/s?

- Would you consider going to the doctor as a couple to get tested? Please explain your reasons.

- When was your last annual physical/check-up?

- If complete blood tests were done please explain the results.

- What is your understanding of the term exclusive?

- At what point in a dating relationship do you believe a couple should date exclusively?

- Do you assume the other person will feel the same way about being exclusive or do you take it upon yourself to communicate your expectations?

- How soon into a relationship do you tend to find yourself sleeping with your partner?

- How long would you *like* to wait before being intimate with your partner? Do you tell them? Please explain.

- When, typically does the conversation of ones' sexual history tend to come up; before or after you have engaged in a physical relationship with them? Please explain.

- Do you feel in control of the physical aspect of your relationships? Please explain.

SEXUALLY TRANSMITTED DISEASES & INFECTIONS

- Describe any situations where you regretted being intimate with someone? Please explain

- Did you seek help from a friend, parent, counselor, pastor or aid worker regarding this? Please explain.

- Do you consider yourself as being sexually active? Please explain.

- What methods of protection do you or did you use, if any?

- Who was responsible for providing them? How did you decide this?

- How did the discussion come about? Who brought it up?

- How do you feel about suggesting the use of protection? Does it make you uncomfortable or fearful of how you may appear to the other person? Please explain

- If so, do you prefer to wait for the other person to suggest it or do you take your own measures? What do you do?

- It is not uncommon for both sexes to fear that they may offend the other party if they suggest protection. Some say they feel that they are insinuating that the other person is a health risk. Please share your thoughts on this?

- What do you think should be the way forward?

- Do you often find yourself giving in to you or your partners' physical needs against your will? Please explain.

- Have you ever paid for sex, if so when and how often?

- If yes, do you still do it? If not, what made you stop and when?

- Have you ever been paid for sex or received gifts in exchange for sex?

- Does this still happen and if not, when did it stop and why?

- Have you ever contracted, been tested for or been treated for any STIs or STD's? Which ones and when?

- If you have any disease, sexually transmitted or otherwise that cannot be cured please explain.

- If you are on any medications or regiments to suppress an outbreak or control the effects of a disease, please explain.

- Are you still under-going any treatment for any sexually transmitted or acquired disease?

- How sure are you at present of all aspects of your health? What medical tests or assessments do you base that on?

- Have you ever disclosed to someone that you had or still have an STI or STD? If so at what stage of the relationship?

- Had you already been intimate with them and if so, had you suggested that they use protection?

- If not, please explain what the events that had occurred and what happened next?

- Has anyone later found out, suspected or even accused you of passing on an infection to them? Explain how you handled the situation and if you had been aware of having an infection or not.

- Has anyone ever disclosed to you that *they* had an STI or STD? If so, at what stage of the relationship?

- Had you already been intimate with them and if so, had either of you suggested or used protection?

- If not, please explain the events that had occurred and what happened after this incident.

- Have you ever found out, suspected or even accused someone of passing on an infection to you? Explain how they handled the situation and whether they had been aware of this or not.

SEXUAL NETWORKS & LIFESTYLES

- Describe your "sexual network/s" including any "friends with benefits" arrangements you have had or still have.

- Are you still sexually involved with your former partner or the parent of your child or children? Please explain.

- If you are or have been sexually active did you or do you always discuss and use contraceptives to prevent unwanted pregnancies and sexually transmitted diseases?

- Have you ever had sexual relations with any persons of the same sex? If so, when and how often?

- How did you asses your level of risk of contracting a sexually transmitted infection or disease? What measures did you take?

- Have you ever participated in an orgy or group sex or swingers groups? If so, when and how often?

- Did you and your partners get tested or use protection? If so what checks were set in place to ensure this?

- For how long and until when did you engage in this lifestyle?

- Have you ever had sexual relations whilst under the influence of drugs, sedatives, alcohol or any mind altering substances? Explain.

- Where you conscious all the time, aware of where you were or whom you were with?

- Are you comfortable with your physical appearance? If not, what would you like to change and why?

- Do you consider yourself to be sexually attractive? Explain.

- As a child did you ever fantasize about being the opposite sex? Please explain.

- Did your fantasies stop? Please explain how and when?

- If they did not stop, did you ever consider or pursue a trans-gender, trans-sexual or homosexual lifestyle? Please explain.

- Did you ever or would you like to undergo a sex change or gender correcting operation? Please explain.

- Have you ever been forced to have relations with anyone against your will? If you are comfortable discussing the situation, please explain what happened.

- Have you ever been the victim or accused of date rape?

- Did you report the incident, seek counselling and get tested? Please explain your answers.

- Is watching or reading pornography a part of your former or current lifestyle? Please explain to what extent.

- Describe any online relationships that are of a romantic or sexual nature. Do you consider them as serious?

- Have you ever cheated or been suspected of cheating in a relationship? Explain how this situation arose and ended.

- Have you ever been cheated on? Explain the circumstances and how you discovered this. What did you do about it?

- Do you know if protection was used during the affair/s?

- If you been unfaithful more than once, please explain.

- Have you ever been accused of being unfaithful? Explain how the accusation came about and if there was an affair?

- Did any of your relationships end because of infidelity? Please explain.

- Did any pregnancies arise from any of your sexual relations? Did/do you dispute your paternity in any of these?

- If so, were any children subsequently born? Is there any question on the paternity of any of them? Explain why.

- If not, were any of these pregnancies terminated? Explain your part or knowledge of this.

- Did any pregnancies result in a miscarriage?

- How did any pregnancies affect your relationships?

- How did the loss of any pregnancies affect you?

- As far as you know, did the termination of any pregnancies affect your ability to have children?

- What measures or recourse did you take to improve your chances of having children in the future?

CHAPTER TEN

RELIGION AND FAITH

In spite of our present persuasions, our spiritual upbringing and level of exposure to religious teachings play a pivotal role in our lives. People will even give it more or less importance in a bid to either impress the other person or make them comfortable and not be intimidated by them.

Fearing possible rejection on the grounds of their beliefs makes people often present themselves as "spiritually adaptable" or flexible unless they are absolutely sure of the other person's spiritual requirements.

Yet our beliefs define us. At the core of every being is the present belief system they have chosen. Their beliefs define and guide them until they are presented with and choose a different or modified set of beliefs. They provide a compass that either delineates specific rules or standards to adopt, and when vague, some framework within which to make a decision.

Coupled with their conscience, the individual now has a fairly predictable approach to situations and routine decision making processes. Therefore establishing a fair deal of commonality in spiritual matters can make a couples' approach to issues more harmonious and predictable.

It holds no guarantees as people often change and life changing experiences affect our belief and value system the most. However, for the unexpected things in life, it does help when two peoples' thought processes and moral compasses are not at polarities. Naturally exceptions exist.

A mistake often made is the assumption that if both persons are from the same religion, faith or even denomination, they will share the exact same spiritual perspectives. Therefore leading to less contention and arguing as they will literally see things the same way.

To a certain extent this may hold true, but if two siblings raised in the same house, with the same rules and belief systems can fight and be at variance with each other, what more people raised in different homes, or parts of the world?

Be mindful of this fact when reading this book. Do not unnecessarily overlook certain questions because you would like to assume the answers for your partner based on their upbringing or beliefs. You may not need to ask *every* single question in here but at least consider them. There is a reason why each question is in here.

Consider this, for example, some people convert to religion after having lived a very different life. Understanding where they are coming from will help you assist them in their present struggles. If you knew they had struggled with certain addictions, tendencies, habits etc. you would be a more effective partner when you are prepared to help. You may believe in forgiving the past and in new beginnings but consider how much more effective and supportive you would be if only you knew.

The partner of a former gambling addict would not knowingly relinquish all the family finances into their hands. They may help rehabilitate them by making them responsible over small parts of the budget or even non-monetary issues entirely.

This is possible when they understand what battles have been fought and are ready and willing for what challenges lie ahead. Some things need not be surprises!

Surprises may lie in more subtle issues. Within various religions you may find different degrees of adherence to teachings on attendance, money, contributions, ceremonial practices and celebrations, marital rites, sex before marriage, during periods of fasting and after childbirth, preparation of food, etc. Some families and communities make their own adaptations or take certain liberties that may be surprising to those who are not a part of it.

Having a different opinion is not a negative thing in itself but may be expressed as such when it contradicts the other persons' values. It is very likely that you will challenge each other to think differently. Or persuade each other to adopt a new revelation or aspect of your beliefs. Tolerance is vital but to avoid being vexed and having your beliefs shaken to the very core, you need to ask the following.

- How would you define and describe your spiritual life?

- Were you raised in a home, school or place of worship that practiced tithing, offering and giving of sacrifices? Please explain.

- What are your views on tithing (giving a tenth of your income)?

- Do you tithe, and if so, what percent of your income, or how do you arrive at your amount? If not, why not?

- Would you be agreeable to your spouse tithing? Explain.

- If so, what percent would you find to be agreeable for them to tithe?

- What other monetary and non-monetary contributions or donations to you make to houses of faith or religious ministries?

- What are your views on volunteering in such places?

- Where you raised in a home, school or place of worship that taught prayer? Describe your experiences.

- Describe your regular prayer or meditation routine

- What are your views on praying together as a couple?

- If fasting is a part of your spiritual lifestyle, please explain your experiences with it and how you go about it.

- What are your views on sexual activities between couples when fasting? Explain how strongly you may or may not feel about this.

- How do you determine which matters to pray about and leave to God and which ones to handle on your own?

- Should you and your partner not agree on this who do you believe should make the final determination and how?

- What do you believe is the spiritual role of the husband in a marriage? What does this mean to you?

- What do you believe is the spiritual role of the wife in a marriage? What does this mean to you?

- Describe the spiritual or religious lifestyle you desire to have with your future family

- Where you raised in a home, school or place of worship that taught reading religious literature or writings? Describe your experiences.

- Describe the different religions or spiritual practices you have witnessed, participated in or actively engaged in.

- Describe your experiences with superstition.

- Explain your beliefs on the devil, demons, ghosts, evil powers, evil presences, curses, witchcraft etc. Describe any experiences you may have had with any of them

- Explain your perspective and experiences with astrology.

- Describe any experiences you may have had with psychics, clairvoyants, tarot card readers, fortune tellers etc.

- Describe any experiences you may have had with any prophets or prophecies.

- Would you consider a vocation as a spiritual leader, minister, pastor or priest? Or whichever title is relevant?

- If your spouse was considering such a vocation what would be your position on this?

- If your child was considering such a vocation what would be your position on this?

- Would you ever seriously consider counseling for your own personal development or for your relationship?

- What role would you like your spiritual leaders to have in your future relationship?

- Explain your thoughts on couples' therapy, counselling and marriage seminars.

CHAPTER ELEVEN

EMBRACE THE CHANGE

Remember that ideally, in marriage and long term commitments or relationships, couples should strive to not take each other for granted. Everyone changes over time. Just as our taste in clothes, food, drink, places, social groups, friends and even churches change over time, we must allow for the special people in our lives to also evolve. Let us allow them to grow into new preferences and not hold them hostage to who they were when we met them.

So many couples fail to keep up with or even simply accommodate each other's' growth. They feel cheated and would rather end the relationship than embrace change and accept that even *they* too have changed and that it isn't always a bad thing. Just as preferences change several times during a lifetime so does the direction we take in many areas of our lives.

All people change gradually or rapidly but we can eliminate the chances of discovering this in an unpleasant way. We can do so by asking timely, pertinent questions and being in the right mind-set to embrace the change.

Reflect on what you both have shared and then allow yourselves to be in awe of each other. Acknowledge each other for dealing with the past or even overcoming despair, heartaches, heartbreaks, abuse, derailment of dreams and ambitions and all sorts of challenges.

Then what if after all this one of you chooses to leave the relationship? Let them. Consider the possibility of staying in a relationship which you now know is not right for you. How can you truly commit? You could take your dissatisfaction out on the other person because you expect them to **make** you happy in return for staying. That is a great burden to place on any being.

Discuss your concerns and realize that if you choose to leave the relationship based on what you have learnt it's about **you** not the other person. It is YOU and not them that have the issue. They may be able to live with all this whereas you may not be able to. That does not make either of you bad people.

So avoid making them feel responsible for your choice to end it, if you do. If they choose to end the relationship, try not to see it as a punishment for your past. Try to accept that they had the right to choose whether they can or cannot handle the truth.

YOUR PARTNER IS A SURVIVOR, CELEBRATE THEM!

Remember, life may have been cruel to your partner so avoid causing more hurt by being insensitive, judgmental, interrogating them, being mean, hurtful, , cynical or untrustworthy; just because you can't handle their truth.

So what if in your quest for a stronger bond you;

- You find some uncomfortable truths? Embrace them.

- What if you feel cheated? Forgive.

- Overwhelmed and confused? Pray. Meditate.

If after all this you cannot live with the entirety of your loved ones' past, present and future then admit it. It's **your** failure to accept their truth, not theirs to meet your expectations. Then be a person of honor and keep their secrets till your death, but all the while celebrating *them*.

For every day you and your loved one open your eyes to a brand new dawn, you must celebrate surviving your yesterdays and your yester nights. If you or they are here today, well say a prayer, sing a song, pop a cork, blow up some balloons, turn up the radio, do a jive and do what you have to do to get your celebration spirit in gear!

You have both survived everything that life has hurled at you from the womb till today!

A good book to read if the thought of being alone daunts you is *Married, Single and Divorced* by Dr. Myles Munroe. This book allows your mind to stroll down other corridors that show the amazing possibilities of your life ahead.

I also strongly recommend his teachings on the *Benefits on Being Single*. This book gives a diverse selection of things that single people have the advantage to do. You may definitely have time to do them now; travelling, learning a foreign language, supporting parents, taking a course, the list only opens up your mind to more.

Celebrate your singleness. Merely enduring it until you find another relationship is to short change yourself of a great stage to rest your mind, values, finances etc.

CHAPTER TWELVE

CONCLUSION

At best, the thought of unearthing all the history and experiences that have shaped and defined both your lives, values, principles and ambitions may seem daunting at this stage. Then perhaps the realization that there may be some unpleasant truths behind the questions that you both need to have answered may have given you sleepless nights.

Eventually the fear of facing and embracing the hidden truths beneath the questions may seem more hazardous to the relationship than the seeming reality of what you have. You could just read this book and wonder about what you don't know. Or you could seek to understand yourself and appreciate your partner better in the light of what you both have survived?

If your fear of the unknown and your fear of rocking this boat still overwhelm you, consider this, that the end of **every** love relationship is painful. Be it that the other person chooses to end the relationship unexpectedly, or it ends before one of you is willing to give up; or because the absence endured in a long distance relationship has taken its toll, or the feelings have changed or the other has died.

Any action that signals the summarily end of a relationship results in some pain or disappointment for at least one of you.

Yet knowing this full well, we still embark on the journey of love. We fully embrace the opportunity to grow in significance and vulnerability in another persons' life. We do so without weighing the imminent joys against the inevitable pain at the end of it all. Why?

The good times and memories make the bad times worth it. When we see how we become better in some ways when we are in love we constantly yearn for it. We start to dream bigger, work harder, write poetry, become romantic, care for another, enjoy human touch, and simply live wholly. Until it ends.

Bitter sweet memories and tears are shared but we wouldn't change much for the opportunity to have given our best and loved beyond our previous capacity. We recover from the pain only to become sentimental, try harder than the last relationship, become even more sentimental and forgive without keeping count; all because we felt honored that love has chosen us and found us. Again.

ℱOR ℬETTER OR ℳORSE!

If, however, you both choose to stay, and make a better relationship out of your union then do so while celebrating each other. Celebrate your partner, their ability to share all this with you. Celebrate *your* ability to trust, perhaps, again. Fully embrace the new fold opportunity to see more value and worth in your loved one and even in yourself.

For the married folks, do not be afraid to ask for help or to admit you are struggling. Your success will be sweeter when you make it. Get counseling. More people do than you may think. Confide in your pastors or spiritual elders. Find a couple that you both love and respect to guide you through any difficult phases.

Trust God to heal the past. Then use it only as a reference point to encourage yourself and motivate others. Trust God to place the right people in your present, because He alone knows your future. Then don't wait a **whole long year** to celebrate your anniversary, your existence, your love. Pick random days in the year to celebrate and appreciate each other.

Finally, when you have found your life partner and have weathered some storms and have awesome stories to share, go mentor and guide some young people. This old fashioned yet revolutionary way of dating works. Start them early on this path so that they can see how their present lifestyles may have consequences in the future.

Open up your relationship to them without violating each other's trust. Show them how to grow in love and how to forgive even when it isn't easy. Show them how some things need not be surprises in life. Give the gift of this book and workbook and spread the love.

MAY THE GOD ALMIGHTY

WHO IS LOVE,

BLESS YOU WITH A GREATER CAPACITY

TO LOVE,

FORGIVE

AND TO BE LOVED

AND FORGIVEN.

© 2015

BUT IF IN ALL TIME ONE COULD CONVINCE ME

THAT TO BE LOVED IS BUT THE MOST EXCITING

PASSION TO FEEL IN ALL THE EARTH,

I CAN, AND MUST DO FAR BETTER

TO MAKE THEM BELIEVE,

THAT TO LOVE, EXCEEDS ALL ELSE

IN ITS TOTALITY.

TO LOVE UNRESERVEDLY

AND TO GIVE OF ONESELF

WITHOUT THOUGHT AT ALL TIMES...

TIS FREEDOM INDEED

1993